Cyber Security and Enterprise SIEM tools

Mark Hayward

Published by Mark Hayward, 2025.

Table of Contents

Cyber Security and Enterprise SIEM tools

About

   With over 23 years of cyber security expertise honed as a veteran of the UK Armed Forces, this author stands out as a leading authority on protecting digital landscapes. Their impressive career spans service within both independent roles and esteemed organizations, specifically providing top-tier cyber security solutions to local and central government departments. This unique fusion of military discipline and industry knowledge enables them to simplify complex concepts, making them accessible and engaging for a diverse audience.

Table of Contents

1. Introduction to Cyber Security and SIEM

2. Understanding Security Information and Event Management (SIEM)

3. Selecting the Right SIEM Tool

4. Implementing SIEM Solutions

5. Configuring SIEM for Enterprise Needs

6. Threat Detection and Incident Response

7. Compliance and Regulatory Considerations

8. Analyzing Security Incidents

1. Introduction to Cyber Security and SIEM

1.1. Defining Cyber Security

Cyber security is essential in today's digital world, where organizations increasingly rely on technology to store and manage sensitive information. The concept revolves around protecting networks, systems, and data from cyber threats that can lead to unauthorized access, data breaches, and significant financial losses. With the rise of the Internet of Things (IoT), mobile devices, and remote work, organizations face an expanding attack surface that necessitates a comprehensive security strategy. Cyber security not only involves the implementation of technology and processes to defend digital assets but also the cultivation of a security-aware culture within the organization. This is critical for minimizing risks associated with human error, which is often a key factor in successful cyber attacks. By prioritizing cyber security measures, organizations can safeguard their data, maintain customer trust, and ensure compliance with regulatory standards.

Organizations face a myriad of threats and vulnerabilities in the cyber domain, which can compromise their security posture. Common types of threats include malware, phishing attacks, ransomware, and distributed denial-of-service (DDoS) attacks, each with distinct characteristics and potential impacts. Malware, for instance, can corrupt systems and steal data, while phishing scams trick employees into divulging sensitive information through seemingly legitimate communications. Additionally, vulnerabilities in software, outdated hardware, and weak passwords can serve as gateways for attackers. Understanding these threats and vulnerabilities enables organizations to implement more effective cyber defense strategies. Continuous monitoring for unusual activity, regular software updates, and employee training are vital elements in a proactive security approach. Recognizing that threats evolve rapidly, it is crucial for cyber security professionals to remain vigilant and adaptable in their defense tactics.

Establishing a robust cyber security framework requires a multi-faceted approach that integrates both technological defenses and human factors. Cyber security professionals should focus on creating layered security strategies, often referred to as defense in depth. This approach employs various methods, such as firewalls, intrusion detection systems, and encryption, to create multiple barriers against potential threats. Moreover, fostering a culture of security awareness among employees is equally important, as they are often the first line of defense. Conducting regular training sessions to educate staff about the latest threats and safe practices can significantly reduce risks. Collaboration across departments is essential for creating a comprehensive strategy that addresses security from both a network and individual perspective, ensuring that all aspects of the organization are aligned in the fight against cyber threats.

1.2. Introduction to SIEM Technologies

Security Information and Event Management, commonly referred to as SIEM, plays a critical role in the cybersecurity landscape. SIEM technologies enable organizations to collect, analyze, and act upon vast amounts of security data in real-time. By aggregating log and event data from various sources such as network devices, servers, domain controllers, and applications, SIEM ensures that security teams have a centralized view of their security posture. The primary purpose of SIEM is to provide timely detection of incidents, streamline compliance reporting, and improve the overall efficiency of security operations. With the increasing sophistication of cyber threats, the need for a robust SIEM solution has never been greater.

SIEM tools are designed to seamlessly aggregate data from a wide variety of sources, consolidating this information into a single, manageable dashboard. This integration includes data feeds from firewalls, intrusion detection systems, antivirus software, and even user activity logs. Once the data is collected, SIEM utilizes advanced analytics and correlation rules to identify potential security incidents. This process not only helps in detecting anomalies but also in tracing the origin of threats, allowing security professionals to respond effectively and efficiently. The capability of SIEM to facilitate real-time monitoring and historical data analysis is invaluable for any organization looking to enhance its security posture and mitigate risks effectively.

For organizations eager to bolster their cybersecurity frameworks, investing in a SIEM solution that aligns with their specific needs and infrastructure can be transformative. By automating the aggregation and analysis of security data, businesses can elevate their threat detection capabilities and strengthen their incident response strategies, ensuring a proactive stance against evolving cyber threats.

1.3. Importance of SIEM in Modern Enterprises

Security Information and Event Management (SIEM) plays a crucial role in enhancing the security posture of enterprises by providing real-time analysis and monitoring of security alerts generated by hardware and applications. By aggregating and correlating data from various sources, including servers, network devices, and security appliances, SIEM systems empower organizations to detect threats more effectively and respond to incidents in a timely manner. This capability is vital in today's landscape, where cyber threats are becoming increasingly sophisticated and frequent. Cybersecurity professionals rely on SIEM not only for proactive threat detection but also for compliance reporting and historical data analysis. The ability to centralize security monitoring means that teams can streamline their operations, sharing information quickly and accurately, which is essential when orchestrating a coordinated response to incidents.

Numerous case studies illustrate the importance of SIEM in mitigating security risks. For instance, a financial institution implemented a SIEM solution that allowed it to monitor user behaviors across its network. By setting up custom alerts based on unusual login patterns, the organization was able to quickly identify and respond to a series of unauthorized access attempts. This timely intervention helped to prevent potential breaches and saved the institution from significant financial loss as well as reputational damage. Similarly, a healthcare provider leveraged SIEM to ensure compliance with regulations like HIPAA by continuously monitoring for the unauthorized access of patient records. The system detected suspicious activities that enabled investigators to act before any data loss could occur. These examples underscore how SIEM can be not just a reactive tool but a proactive measure that enhances overall security and compliance in enterprises.

Integrating SIEM effectively within an organization also emphasizes the importance of continuous tuning and optimization of the system. Organizations are encouraged to regularly review their security policies, adjust the parameters of their SIEM tools in response to evolving threats, and provide ongoing training for their staff. For security professionals, understanding the intricacies of their specific SIEM solution is key to maximizing its potential. They should leverage the insights gained from historical data within the SIEM to refine their threat detection capabilities continually. Engaging in regular threat assessments can help identify gaps in security, allowing enterprises to stay ahead of cybercriminals.

2. Understanding Security Information and Event Management (SIEM)

2.1. Components of SIEM Systems

Examining the core elements that make up a SIEM solution reveals that a comprehensive Security Information and Event Management (SIEM) system consists of several critical components. The most fundamental part of a SIEM solution is the data collection module, which gathers logs and events from various sources across the organization's network. This includes servers, firewalls, intrusion detection systems, and other devices. The ability to aggregate and normalize data in real-time is vital, as it ensures consistent interpretation of log entries regardless of their origin. Next, the data storage component plays a crucial role in retaining this information for further analysis. Proper storage will not only facilitate immediate responses but also allow for forensic investigations and compliance with regulatory requirements. Additionally, the correlation engine serves as the brain of the SIEM, analyzing aggregated data to identify patterns indicative of security incidents. This correlation is what transforms raw data into actionable intelligence, allowing organizations to respond to potential threats swiftly.

Understanding how these components work together to provide comprehensive security monitoring is essential for any cybersecurity professional. The integration of data collection, storage, and correlation capabilities means that a SIEM can provide a holistic view of the security landscape. When an organization implements a SIEM, it establishes a continuous feedback loop; data is collected, analyzed, and acted upon almost instantaneously. Through real-time alerting and reporting, security teams can monitor suspicious activity and react proactively. The collaborative role of user behavior analytics, threat intelligence feeds, and security alert management enhances the effectiveness of the SIEM. These components work symbiotically, ensuring that an organization not only detects incidents but also understands them in context. By correlating multiple data points from various sources, SIEM systems can uncover sophisticated attack patterns that might otherwise remain obscured.

For organizations looking to enhance workplace security, it's essential to prioritize the seamless integration of these core components. A well-implemented SIEM provides improved detection capabilities and incident response timelines. Cybersecurity professionals should continually assess and optimize their SIEM systems, ensuring that all components work in unison. Regularly updating threat intelligence feeds and refining correlation rules can significantly enhance operational effectiveness. Furthermore, thorough training for security analysts on the functionalities of the SIEM fosters a proactive security culture, enabling teams to maximize the potential of their investment in these critical systems.

2.2. How SIEM Works

SIEM solutions collect a diverse array of data from various sources within an organization's network infrastructure. This includes logs from firewalls, intrusion detection systems, servers, and applications. The data collection process occurs in real-time, allowing for the aggregation of large amounts of information, which is essential for effective monitoring. Once data has been collected, it undergoes a crucial normalization process. Normalization transforms the vast array of data formats into a consistent format that facilitates easier analysis. By standardizing log data, SIEM systems improve the ability to correlate events and detect patterns of suspicious activity across various systems and devices. Correlation is particularly important, as it enables the SIEM to identify relationships between disparate events, which could indicate a security threat or breach. This process leverages sophisticated algorithms and rule sets to pinpoint anomalies and provide a clearer picture of network activity.

When the SIEM identifies deviations from expected behavior or thresholds, it generates alerts to notify security personnel of potential security incidents. These alerts can be prioritized based on the severity of the detected anomaly and the contextual importance of the asset involved. For instance, unusual access patterns on a sensitive database would trigger a higher alert priority than anomalies detected on less critical systems. Additionally, alerts can be refined based on factors like user behavior analytics, which assess whether an individual's actions align with their normal patterns. Correlating this behavioral information with broader dataset trends enhances the accuracy of alerts. It's essential for cybersecurity teams to fine-tune these settings to reduce false positives and focus attention on genuine threats. Integrating machine learning techniques can also improve the detection of sophisticated threats by continuously learning from new data and adapting to evolving security patterns, ultimately providing a more robust defense strategy for the organization.

Proactive implementation of SIEM requires continuous monitoring and adjustment of data collection and alert generation strategies. Regularly reviewing the rules and thresholds that govern alert generation will ensure the SIEM remains effective against emerging threats. Tailoring the correlation rules to match the specific environment and risk profile of an organization greatly enhances the ability to detect and respond to incidents swiftly. Therefore, it's advisable for organizations to engage in periodic assessments and implement feedback loops that allow security teams to refine their alerting processes. Effective use of SIEM not only aids in immediate threat detection but also contributes to a comprehensive understanding of the organization's security posture over time.

2.3. Types of Events Collected by SIEM

SIEM systems are designed to aggregate and analyze log and event data from multiple sources across an organization's IT infrastructure. The diversity of this data is crucial, as it encompasses everything from system logs and network traffic to security events and application activities. Common types of logs collected by SIEM include firewall logs, intrusion detection system (IDS) alerts, antivirus logs, operating system logs, and database logs. Additionally, data from endpoints, such as user workstations and servers, are vital as they provide insights into user behavior and potential security incidents. This vast array of event data allows SIEM systems to correlate activities, identify anomalies, and respond to potential threats in real time, thereby enhancing situational awareness for security teams. The ability to incorporate data from cloud services and third-party applications is also increasingly important as organizations expand their digital landscapes.

Understanding the significance of different event types is critical for effective security monitoring. Each event carries specific contextual information that helps security professionals assess potential risks. For instance, a failed login attempt may stem from a legitimate user mistyping their password, or it could indicate a targeted attack on user credentials. Similarly, changes to user permissions might signal a benign administrative task or an unauthorized escalation of privileges, highlighting the importance of context in evaluating events. By leveraging the capabilities of a SIEM to prioritize and analyze these events, organizations can better allocate resources to tackle genuine threats while minimizing false positives. This nuanced understanding not only aids in effective incident response but also helps in compliance reporting for various regulations, showcasing a proactive approach to security.

Investing time in developing a comprehensive event classification and response strategy is paramount. Each organization should conduct a thorough assessment of their specific environment, identifying which events require immediate attention and which can be monitored passively. Setting up alerts for critical and high-severity events enables security teams to act swiftly, while the monitoring of lower-severity events can provide a broader understanding of the security posture over time. Maintaining a regular review of the types of events collected and their significance is essential as the threat landscape evolves, ensuring that the SIEM remains an effective tool in safeguarding organizational assets.

3. Selecting the Right SIEM Tool

3.1. Key Features to Consider

When selecting a security solution, it is imperative to focus on crucial features that can greatly enhance your organization's defense mechanisms. Event correlation is one of the top features to seek. This capability allows the system to analyze logs and security events from various sources in real-time, connecting seemingly unrelated incidents to unveil potential threats. Real-time monitoring is similarly critical; it provides immediate insight into network activities and alerts security personnel of suspicious behavior as it unfolds. The ability to generate comprehensive reporting is also essential. Effective reporting capabilities not only track incidents but also assess the overall security posture, enabling organizations to meet compliance regulations and refine their security strategies over time.

Another important aspect to evaluate is scalability and integration, as these factors significantly influence the long-term effectiveness of a security solution. As organizations grow, their security needs evolve, requiring solutions that can scale in response to increased data loads and complex environments. A solution that integrates seamlessly with existing tools and platforms not only reduces operational disruption but also maximizes the value of current technology investments. This integration ensures that security measures can adapt to new threats without necessitating a complete overhaul of the existing infrastructure, ultimately safeguarding the organization's resources and enhancing its resilience against cyber-attacks.

Consider implementing systems that feature automation capabilities. By automating routine security tasks, such as patch management and threat detection, cybersecurity professionals can devote more time to strategic initiatives. This shift not only optimizes workforce efficiency but also reduces the chances of human error, which is a frequent vulnerability in security practices. Always remember that the best security solutions are those that foster an ongoing evolution of security practices to stay ahead in the ever-changing landscape of cyber threats.

3.2. Vendor Comparison

Comparing top Security Information and Event Management (SIEM) vendors involves a thorough examination of their market presence and the range of offerings they provide. The leading players in the SIEM market typically include names like Splunk, IBM QRadar, ArcSight, and LogRhythm, among others. These vendors are recognized for their robust capabilities in threat detection, incident response, and compliance monitoring. Market presence is often gauged through factors such as market share, customer base, and the ability to innovate in response to the evolving landscape of cyber threats. While one vendor may dominate in enterprise-scale solutions, another might shine in integration capabilities or niche markets. Understanding the nuances of each SIEM solution is critical, as it allows cybersecurity professionals to align their specific needs with the right vendor. For instance, while a system that offers extensive analytics and reporting may be appealing, it is vital to ensure that it also comes with user-friendly features and seamless integration with existing infrastructure.

Utilizing customer feedback and industry reviews can greatly assist in assessing vendor reliability. Many cybersecurity professionals turn to platforms offering peer reviews and ratings to gather insights regarding user experiences. These reviews can highlight strengths and weaknesses that aren't always evident from marketing materials. Features such as customer support responsiveness, ease of implementation, and overall satisfaction levels provide valuable information that can significantly influence purchasing decisions. Furthermore, engaging with the professional community through forums and discussions about the experiences with different SIEM vendors can uncover practical insights that formal reviews may overlook. When evaluating customer feedback, attention should also be paid to how vendors have addressed past issues, as this demonstrates their commitment to user experience and continuous improvement.

To enhance decision-making, consider conducting a proof of concept (POC) with vendors of interest. This hands-on approach allows organizations to evaluate the product in real-world scenarios and assess how well it meets their specific security needs. Choosing the right SIEM vendor goes beyond just product capabilities; it involves understanding the vendor's roadmap, commitment to security innovation, and alignment with your organization's long-term objectives. By approaching the vendor comparison process systematically, cybersecurity professionals can secure the buy-in from stakeholders, ensuring alignment with organizational goals while enhancing overall workplace security.

3.3. Total Cost of Ownership

Understanding the total cost of ownership (TCO) of a Security Information and Event Management (SIEM) solution is crucial for cyber security professionals. The costs associated with purchasing and maintaining a SIEM extend far beyond the initial software license. Organizations must consider hardware purchases, ongoing maintenance fees, and the costs related to system upgrades. These factors combine to shape a more accurate view of what investing in a SIEM solution truly entails. Additionally, labor costs must be factored in, as skilled personnel are required to manage the solution effectively. This includes not only trained cyber security analysts who can interpret the data generated by the SIEM but also engineers who maintain and troubleshoot the system. The utilities involved in running the hardware, such as electricity and climate control, also contribute to the overall expenditure. Organizations should take a comprehensive approach to budgeting for a SIEM, ensuring that all facets of ownership are carefully analyzed.

Hidden costs associated with SIEM solutions can significantly impact the TCO and may not be evident during initial evaluations. For example, integration expenses can arise when trying to connect the SIEM to existing security infrastructure or third-party applications. This integration often requires specialized skills and can lead to increased project timelines and unforeseen expenses. Moreover, the ongoing cost of upgrades and the need for continuous updates to protect against emerging threats must also be considered. Failure to account for future scalability presents another risk. As a business grows, its security needs will evolve, necessitating advancements in the SIEM solution that may require substantial additional investment. Buying into a SIEM without understanding these complexities can lead to unexpected budget overruns and resource shortages.

When evaluating the TCO for a SIEM solution, cyber security professionals should endeavor to account for both visible and hidden costs to ensure informed decision-making. This comprehensive analysis will assist in gaining buy-in from company executives, as they seek to understand the real implications of the investment. A detailed cost breakdown can facilitate discussions about return on investment and the potential risk mitigation benefits that a well-implemented SIEM can provide. By approaching financial planning from multiple angles, organizations can optimize their cyber security budgets and ensure that their security postures remain robust and agile in an ever-evolving threat landscape.

4. Implementing SIEM Solutions

4.1. Planning the Implementation

Establishing a robust roadmap is crucial for the successful deployment of a Security Information and Event Management (SIEM) system within your organization. The journey begins with assessing your current security posture and identifying specific goals that align with your business objectives. A well-defined roadmap should encompass clear stages such as requirements gathering, system selection, deployment, integration, and continuous improvement. Each stage must include defined metrics for measuring success, ensuring that the chosen SIEM solution aligns with your organization's needs and regulatory compliance requirements. Additionally, it's important to account for potential challenges during the rollout, such as the integration of existing systems and managing user expectations. Considering a phased implementation approach can facilitate smoother transitions, allowing teams to adapt to the new tools and practices gradually, which can significantly reduce resistance and increase buy-in across departments.

Identifying stakeholders early in the implementation process is critical to ensuring alignment and support across different levels of the organization. Stakeholders typically include IT staff, network security professionals, compliance officers, and executive leadership. Each stakeholder role should be clearly outlined to avoid overlaps and gaps in responsibility. For instance, while the IT team may be tasked with system installation and configuration, network security professionals can focus on monitoring and responding to security incidents through the SIEM. Including executive leadership can further facilitate necessary resources and strategic direction, helping to articulate the value of the SIEM to the wider business. It is advisable to cultivate a culture of collaboration among stakeholders by holding regular meetings that focus on sharing progress, discussing challenges, and iterating the implementation strategies. The more informed each stakeholder feels, the better the chances of achieving a successful SIEM rollout.

In the phase of planning your SIEM implementation, it's beneficial to involve all relevant parties early and often. Building a strong communication plan will enable stakeholders to stay informed about project updates, timelines, and expectations. Consider using project management tools that allow for visibility throughout the implementation process. Regular reporting not only keeps everyone on track but also reinforces a sense of accountability, ultimately supporting your overall objectives. Keep in mind that the successful deployment of a SIEM is not merely a technical endeavor; it is also a cultural shift within your organization. Creating a supportive environment that encourages teamwork can pave the way for more efficient incident response, improved threat management, and, ultimately, a more secure organizational framework. Recognizing and addressing the party's needs while fostering a culture of joint effort will be instrumental in achieving an effective and resilient security stance.

4.2. Integration with Existing Systems

Integrating a Security Information and Event Management (SIEM) system into existing IT and security infrastructures requires a strategic approach that considers both technical and operational best practices. Firstly, it is essential to evaluate the current architecture and identify how the SIEM can complement existing security tools rather than replace them. This involves mapping out data flow between systems, understanding data formats, and ensuring compatibility with current security protocols. A phased integration can be beneficial; starting with pilot projects allows for testing and refining processes before a full rollout. Collaboration among teams is crucial, as engagement from network engineers, security analysts, and system owners ensures that all stakeholders are on the same page and that their input is factored into the integration plan.

Despite the advantages, integrating SIEM systems is not without its challenges. Common obstacles include data overload, where the SIEM captures too much information, leading to analysis paralysis and diminishing the system's efficacy. Organizations often face integration hurdles due to incompatible data sources or outdated technologies. To address these issues, prioritize critical data sources essential for monitoring and analysis, and establish clear guidelines for what data should be collected. Developing a robust onboarding process for new data sources and regular tuning of the SIEM will improve relevance and response times. Additionally, ensuring that there is a continuous feedback loop to refine collection policies based on ongoing threat assessments is vital.

Both planning and execution stages should include a thorough review of compliance and regulatory issues to ensure that the integration does not inadvertently lead to violations. Communication with stakeholders, particularly upper management and the CEO, during these phases is crucial for obtaining necessary approvals and resources. Presenting the integration as a foundational element of the organization's wider security strategy can help secure buy-in from executive leadership. Ultimately, embracing a mindset of continuous improvement and adaptability can make SIEM integration smoother and more effective, allowing cyber security teams to respond to threats proactively.

4.3. Data Sources and Ingestion

Identifying critical data sources is essential for the effective operation of Security Information and Event Management (SIEM) systems. The landscape of cybersecurity threats is continuously evolving, emphasizing the need for comprehensive visibility across diverse assets. Key data sources include network logs from firewalls, intrusion detection systems, and routers, as well as endpoint telemetry from antivirus solutions and endpoint detection tools. Application logs, user authentication records, and cloud service logs also serve valuable roles in painting a complete picture of the organization's security posture. By integrating data from these sources, security teams can establish a robust baseline of normal activity, facilitating the identification of anomalies and potential threats. Investing time in mapping out critical data sources not only enhances incident response times but also aligns security metrics with organizational objectives, fostering a culture of proactive risk management.

Data ingestion methods significantly influence the effectiveness of detection capabilities within SIEM systems. Various techniques exist, including batch ingestion, real-time streaming, and event-driven architectures. Batch ingestion, while easier to manage, may lead to delays in visibility, causing incidents to go undetected for longer periods. On the other hand, real-time streaming provides immediate access to data, which is crucial for timely alerts and rapid response. This approach allows analysts to monitor threats as they occur, significantly improving the organization's ability to mitigate risks. Moreover, event-driven architectures promote a more agile data handling process, enabling automatic responses to specific trigger events, which can reduce the workload on security personnel. Choosing the right ingestion method will depend on the organization's maturity in security operations, regulatory requirements, and the criticality of the systems involved.

Fostering a synergy between data sources and ingestion methods can propel an organization's cybersecurity measure to new heights. Security teams must not only consider the types of data they need but also prioritize how that data is collected and processed. By employing a combination of real-time ingestion methods and integrating diverse data sources, organizations can enhance their situational awareness and expedite detection capabilities. Additionally, regular audits of the data integration process will ensure that it remains optimal and aligned with evolving security needs. As a practical tip, consider conducting a periodic review of your data sources to ensure that new technologies and threats are adequately addressed in your SIEM strategy.

5. Configuring SIEM for Enterprise Needs

5.1. Setting Up Alerts and Thresholds

Establishing clear criteria for alerts is crucial for enabling timely responses to security incidents. Organizations must set parameters that not only define what constitutes an alert but also prioritize incidents based on severity and context. This involves analyzing past incidents to identify patterns and triggers that resulted in breaches or near misses. By doing this, decision-makers can create a tailored alert framework that elevates significant incidents and ensures that security personnel can react promptly. Factors such as the type of threat, asset sensitivity, and operational impact should be included in the criteria to guarantee a comprehensive understanding of potential risks. Using this data-driven approach helps organizations focus their resources on the most critical alerts, ensuring that every incident is assessed and addressed swiftly.

Customizing thresholds is an essential aspect of enhancing the relevancy of alerts and reducing the occurrence of false positives. Different environments will have distinct operational baselines, and arbitrary thresholds may not provide accurate insights into security posture. Tailoring thresholds to specific systems, user behaviors, and business dynamics is imperative. For instance, understanding normal network traffic patterns allows security teams to set dynamic thresholds that alert them only when deviations significantly exceed expected values. This customization not only makes alerts more relevant but also helps prevent alert fatigue, where security professionals become desensitized to notifications due to the volume of irrelevant alerts. Regular reviews of threshold settings based on evolving threats and business changes are essential to maintain their effectiveness.

Maintaining an adaptive alert and threshold strategy is vital in a dynamic threat landscape. Continuous monitoring, coupled with a responsive adjustment mechanism, enables organizations to stay ahead of potential security incidents. Implementing a feedback loop where insights from previous alerts can refine the criteria and thresholds will lead to a progressively improving security ecosystem. Integrating automated tools to assist in this process can further enhance the efficiency of managing alerts and thresholds. Investing in training for team members on the significance of these systems fosters a more proactive security culture, whereby every individual plays a part in identifying and mitigating risks. Regularly testing and updating these systems enhances resilience, ensuring that the organization can defend against increasingly sophisticated cyber threats.

5.2. Customizing Dashboards

Creating visual dashboards that provide essential insights at a glance involves selecting the right metrics and presenting them in a way that is instantly understandable. The complexity of cybersecurity data can often overwhelm stakeholders, so it's crucial to simplify the presentation. Use clear visuals such as line graphs, pie charts, and heat maps that showcase trends and anomalies. Implementing color coding can further enhance readability, differentiating between safe and risky behaviors at a glance. Aim for dashboards that offer real-time monitoring capabilities, allowing cybersecurity professionals to track active threats and responses effectively. By prioritizing actionable insights, the dashboards become a powerful tool for decision-making, not just data display.

Ensuring that reports cater to different stakeholders' needs for security monitoring requires a comprehensive understanding of who will be using the data. Executives may be more focused on overarching trends and compliance metrics rather than granular technical details. Tailoring reports for different levels within the organization can greatly enhance the effectiveness of communication. For example, technical teams might benefit from in-depth analysis and detailed risk assessments, while non-technical stakeholders may prefer summaries that highlight key risk areas and tangible recommendations.

Utilizing interactive dashboards that allow stakeholders to customize their own views can foster engagement and maintain interest in the security posture of the organization.

It's important to remember that the ultimate goal of these dashboards and reports is to facilitate informed decision-making across the organization. Regularly soliciting feedback from users can guide further customization, ensuring that the dashboards remain relevant and useful. Additionally, providing training on how to interpret the data presented will empower stakeholders to take proactive measures in enhancing security. Emphasizing the strategic importance of these customized dashboards can also aid in gaining CEO buy-in, reinforcing their role as a vital part of organizational resilience against cyber threats.

5.3. User Role and Permission Management

Implementing role-based access control (RBAC) is crucial for securing the functionalities of Security Information and Event Management (SIEM) systems. By defining user roles with specific permissions tailored to job functions, organizations can minimize the risk of unauthorized access to sensitive information. The principle of least privilege should be enforced, allowing users only the access necessary to perform their job tasks. This approach not only enhances security but also streamlines the management of user permissions. In a typical SIEM environment, it is advisable to segment roles clearly, such as Analyst, Administrator, and Viewer, ensuring that users in different roles have distinct access levels. Regular audits of these roles help maintain security posture by identifying and mitigating any discrepancies while also providing insights into user behavior patterns that could indicate potential risks.

Best practices for managing user permissions are essential to safeguarding sensitive data. It is important to regularly review user access levels and adjust them based on changes in personnel or job responsibilities. Implementing automated tools for monitoring access can help detect anomalies in user behavior, which may suggest unauthorized attempts to access sensitive information. Additionally, employing a strict on-boarding and off-boarding process ensures that new employees receive the appropriate permissions from the outset while those who leave the organization are promptly denied access to the systems. Data classification can also play a key role in determining the type of access needed for different users, allowing cyber security teams to enforce stricter controls on high-risk data. Training and awareness programs for employees about the importance of permissions and their role in organizational security can foster a culture of vigilance.

Regularly updating and refining user roles and permissions is vital for adapting to the evolving landscape of threats in cyber security. Establishing clear documentation around role responsibilities and access can simplify audits and compliance efforts. Utilizing advanced technology, such as AI-driven analytics tools, can provide deeper insights into user access patterns and potential vulnerabilities that can be leveraged to fortify security infrastructure. Always ensure that all user role and permission management strategies align with industry standards and regulatory requirements to maintain trust and integrity within the organization. These practices not only protect sensitive information but also enhance overall workplace security, fostering a proactive security culture.

6. Threat Detection and Incident Response

6.1. Real-time Threat Monitoring

Exploring methodologies used for continuous threat surveillance emphasizes the necessity for organizations to adopt a proactive stance in their cybersecurity efforts. Various techniques have emerged to ensure that potential threats are identified and neutralized before they can inflict damage. Behavioral analysis, machine learning, and real-time data analytics are instrumental in recognizing irregular patterns that may signify a security breach. Furthermore, integrating threat intelligence feeds facilitates a broader understanding of the evolving landscape, allowing security teams to adapt their defenses to anticipated attacks. Continuous monitoring requires a robust infrastructure that leverages advanced technologies, including endpoint monitoring solutions and automated incident response systems. This methodology not only enhances detection capabilities but also ensures that security resources are utilized effectively in the fight against cyber threats. By prioritizing continuous threat surveillance, organizations can develop a security framework that is responsive rather than reactive, significantly reducing their vulnerability to attacks.

Discussing the importance of timely alerts in minimizing potential damage underscores the critical need for swift and accurate notifications within the incident response lifecycle. When an anomaly is detected, the urgency of alerting the appropriate personnel cannot be overstated. Instant notifications empower cybersecurity teams to swiftly assess the situation, initiate containment protocols, and mitigate damage before the vulnerability is exploited. The integration of automated alert systems into the security framework not only minimizes response time but also ensures that human error is reduced, allowing for a more systematic approach to incident management. This technology needs to be finely tuned to prevent alert fatigue among the team, as excessive notifications can lead to desensitization. Instead, focusing on actionable insights and prioritizing high-risk alerts will enable professionals to focus on what truly matters. Ensuring that decision-makers receive timely, clear, and relevant alerts is essential for maintaining operational integrity and safeguarding organizational assets.

By leveraging these methodologies and prioritizing timely notifications, organizations will enhance their cybersecurity posture significantly. Regular training and simulations will prepare teams to respond quickly to incidents, reinforcing the importance of a culture geared towards rapid response and resilience. An effective strategy to consider is the establishment of a threat response team that specializes in real-time monitoring and incident analysis. This dedicated approach will not only streamline processes but also foster inter-departmental collaboration, ensuring that all aspects of the business are on the same page when it comes to security. It's vital that cybersecurity professionals convey the urgency of these strategies to CEOs and other executives, illustrating how these measures translate into protecting the company's bottom line. Fostering an environment where cybersecurity is prioritized at every level will ultimately fortify the organization against an ever-changing threat landscape.

6.2. Incident Response Planning

Creating comprehensive incident response plans is vital for effectively handling security breaches. These plans serve as the framework within which organizations can operate during a security incident. It involves identifying potential threats, assessing vulnerabilities, and formulating strategic responses. A well-developed incident response plan outlines specific roles and responsibilities, communication strategies, and escalation procedures, ensuring that everyone understands their part when an incident occurs. The plan should also include a thorough analysis of past incidents to help predict future breaches and improve response strategies. Regularly updating these plans is crucial as the security landscape evolves, ensuring that they remain relevant to the current threat environment. Engaging stakeholders across the organization, including IT, legal, and HR, fosters a culture of security awareness and collaboration, strengthening the overall incident response capability.

Training teams on executing response protocols effectively is equally important. Even the most robust incident response plan is only as good as the people who implement it. Training should involve realistic simulations that mimic potential attack scenarios, allowing team members to practice their responses in a controlled environment. This hands-on experience not only helps identify gaps in the response plan but also builds confidence and competence among team members. Incorporating lessons learned from these exercises into ongoing training ensures continuous improvement. It's advisable to hold regular refresher sessions and update training materials to reflect any changes in technology or procedures. Engaging upper management and ensuring their buy-in can enhance the training initiative, positioning security as a priority across the organization.

Ultimately, the effectiveness of incident response planning and execution lies in a proactive approach that embraces regular evaluation and adjustment. Organizations should foster an environment where feedback is encouraged, and lessons are drawn from both successes and failures. Implementing a culture of transparency around security incidents not only strengthens response strategies but also enhances trust among stakeholders. Building resilience through continuous learning and improvement will ensure that organizations are better prepared when incidents occur. It is crucial to keep the incident response plan accessible and visible within the organization. Regularly testing the plan and refining it based on the most current threats can prevent chaos during an actual breach, significantly mitigating potential damages.

6.3. Case Studies of Threat Detection

Analyzing real-world examples where SIEM tools identified and mitigated threats reveals the critical role these systems play in modern cybersecurity. For instance, at a large financial institution, a SIEM solution detected unusual outbound traffic that indicated potential data exfiltration. By correlating logs from various sources, the SIEM was able to pinpoint the activity to a specific compromised account. The rapid identification allowed the security team to respond promptly, isolating the affected systems and securing sensitive customer data before any real harm could occur. This incident highlights how valuable real-time monitoring and alerts are in safeguarding an organization's assets, especially those involving sensitive information.

Extracting lessons learned from such case studies is vital for improving future detection techniques. Continuous improvement in threat detection mechanisms is necessary as cyber threats evolve rapidly. One key takeaway from the aforementioned case is the importance of integrating machine learning with SIEM systems to enhance anomaly detection capabilities. Organizations began to implement advanced analytics not only to enhance detection rates but also to reduce false positives, allowing security teams to focus on genuine threats. Establishing a feedback loop between analysts and SIEM systems ensures that the systems learn from prior incidents, continuously adapting to current threat landscapes and thereby increasing their efficiency in detecting anomalies.

In addition to technology improvements, fostering a culture of awareness and training among employees is crucial. Regular training sessions on recognizing phishing attempts and other common attack vectors help to mitigate risks at an individual level. By empowering employees with knowledge, companies create a first line of defense that, when coupled with robust monitoring systems, significantly enhances overall security posture. Ensuring that cybersecurity remains everyone's responsibility, from the ground up, not only instills a sense of vigilance but also creates a resilient environment capable of responding effectively to emerging threats.

7. Compliance and Regulatory Considerations

7.1. Understanding Compliance Frameworks

Compliance frameworks play a crucial role in the realm of cybersecurity, acting as a structured guide for organizations to manage their cybersecurity risks. Some of the most recognized frameworks include the National Institute of Standards and Technology Cybersecurity Framework (NIST CSF), the Health Insurance Portability and Accountability Act (HIPAA), the General Data Protection Regulation (GDPR), and the Payment Card Industry Data Security Standard (PCI DSS). These frameworks provide a set of standards, guidelines, and best practices that help organizations protect sensitive information and comply with legal regulations. Adopting a compliance framework allows companies to implement effective policies, enhance their security posture, and demonstrate a commitment to safeguarding customer data. Understanding the nuances of each framework is essential for cybersecurity professionals, as it enables them to tailor their security measures to meet specific regulatory demands while ensuring robust protection against cyber threats.

The impact of non-compliance on organizations can be profound, posing not only financial risks but also substantial damage to reputation. Organizations that fail to adhere to relevant compliance requirements may face hefty fines, legal repercussions, and increased scrutiny from regulatory bodies. Furthermore, non-compliance can lead to costly data breaches, which can result in the loss of sensitive information and erode customer trust. This loss of trust can have long-lasting effects, leading to diminished sales and a weakened competitive position in the market. For cybersecurity professionals, it is important to communicate these risks effectively to executive leadership to secure the necessary funding and support for compliance initiatives. Demonstrating the financial and operational implications of non-compliance helps in gaining buy-in from CEOs and ensuring that security measures are prioritized within the organization.

Efforts to align with compliance frameworks require ongoing commitment and resources from organizations. Cybersecurity professionals should take proactive steps to maintain compliance, such as conducting regular audits, providing employee training, and employing risk management strategies. These practices not only help in staying compliant but also bolster the resilience of the organization's cybersecurity posture. Regular assessments of policies and procedures ensure they remain effective in combating evolving threats and aligning with changing regulations. Promoting a culture of compliance within the workplace can also enhance employee awareness and enable a more robust defense against cyber threats.

7.2. Role of SIEM in Compliance Reporting

Organizations face relentless pressure to comply with various regulatory requirements, and Security Information and Event Management (SIEM) systems play a crucial role in enabling them to meet these demands. SIEM solutions aggregate and analyze security data from across the enterprise, providing real-time visibility into activities that can impact compliance. By collecting logs and data from endpoints, servers, applications, and network devices, SIEM systems help organizations identify potential vulnerabilities, suspicious behaviors, or breaches that could lead to non-compliance. The ability to centralize security information allows compliance teams to streamline their reporting processes, ensuring that they can promptly address regulatory expectations without being overwhelmed by data. This centralized oversight not only aids in identifying compliance gaps but also in enhancing overall security posture.

Any robust SIEM solution comes equipped with a variety of reporting features that significantly streamline compliance processes. These capabilities include automated report generation, which facilitates the creation of documentation necessary for audits and regulatory submissions. Organizations can customize these reports to align with specific regulatory frameworks, such as GDPR, HIPAA, or PCI-DSS, highlighting relevant incidents, trends, and areas of risk. Moreover, built-in dashboards provide visual analytics that convey complex compliance data in an easily digestible format, making it simpler for stakeholders to understand how well the organization is adhering to regulations. This visualization not only aids compliance officers but also supports executive decision-making, capturing the attention of CEOs and board members by presenting clear and actionable insights into compliance status and security health.

Keeping in mind that compliance reporting is not merely a task but a critical component of risk management, organizations should continuously optimize their SIEM configurations to capture the most relevant security events. Cybersecurity professionals, in collaboration with compliance teams, must regularly review reporting parameters to ensure they align with evolving regulatory requirements and internal policies. This proactive adjustment makes it easier to stay ahead of potential non-compliance issues. Embracing automated reporting features and data visualization tools can significantly enhance communication with organizational leadership, reinforcing the importance of a strong cybersecurity foundation in achieving compliance and protecting business integrity.

7.3. Auditing and Continuous Compliance

Regular audits play an essential role in maintaining compliance within any organization. They help ensure that policies and procedures align with security standards, identifying gaps that could potentially expose vulnerabilities. Consistent auditing not only checks adherence to regulations but also boosts the overall security posture of the institution. When compliance is treated as a continuous process rather than an occasional checklist, it fosters a culture of security awareness. This proactive approach allows organizations to respond swiftly to emerging threats, demonstrating to both stakeholders and regulators a commitment to protecting sensitive data. In essence, regular audits are not just a means to an end; they are a fundamental practice in building and sustaining trust with customers, partners, and regulatory bodies. CEOs need to recognize that investing in regular audits can save time and resources in the long run as it mitigates risk and pre-empts costly non-compliance penalties.

Security Information and Event Management (SIEM) systems significantly enhance ongoing compliance efforts by providing real-time analysis of security alerts generated by applications and network hardware. SIEM tools consolidate security data across an organization, enabling IT teams to monitor activities continuously and detect irregularities that may pose compliance risks. The automation of log collection and analysis streamlines the audit process, saving valuable time and reducing human error. By leveraging advanced analytics, SIEM solutions can highlight compliance discrepancies and suggest necessary corrective actions. Moreover, the visibility these systems offer empowers security teams to investigate incidents promptly and comprehensively, ensuring that compliance standards are not only met but also maintained over time. As such, CEOs should see SIEM not merely as a tool but as a crucial framework that fortifies their organization's commitment to continuous compliance.

Continuous compliance is ultimately about integrating security into the fabric of the organization's operations. This can be achieved by fostering collaboration across departments, including legal, IT, and compliance functions, to harmonize their efforts. Tools like SIEM become more effective when supplemented by a culture of accountability where all employees understand their role in maintaining compliance. Regular training and awareness programs are vital to keep everyone informed about compliance standards and security best practices. Organizations should ensure that compliance is not a siloed effort but part of everyday discussions, leading to an atmosphere where security becomes a collective responsibility. A practical tip for Cyber Security professionals is to develop a roadmap that aligns audit schedules with business operations, allowing for flexible adjustments while maintaining necessary rigor in compliance checks.

8. Analyzing Security Incidents

8.1. Forensic Analysis Techniques

Forensic analysis is a crucial component of security incident investigations, acting as the investigative backbone that helps organizations understand what occurred during a security breach. It involves collecting, preserving, and examining data from various sources, including networks, servers, endpoint devices, and even the cloud. By uncovering the details of an incident, such as how attackers gained access, what data was affected, and the methods used to exfiltrate information, forensic analysis not only aids in addressing the immediate threat, it also serves as a vital tool for preventing future incidents. Such analyses can highlight weaknesses in security protocols and systems and provide a clearer picture of threat landscapes that organizations must navigate. Given the growing complexity of cyber threats, possessing robust forensic capabilities is no longer just a luxury but a necessity for maintaining corporate integrity and trust. For leadership, understanding this aspect enables better strategic decisions regarding resource allocation toward security measures.

To effectively conduct forensic examinations, security professionals leverage a variety of tools and methodologies designed to gather evidentiary data systematically and efficiently. These tools encompass digital forensics solutions, threat intelligence platforms, and various data recovery applications. The choice of tools often depends on the type of incident being investigated and the specific systems involved. For instance, software like EnCase and FTK is widely used for disk-level analysis, whereas network forensics tools such as Wireshark help in packet-level inspections, allowing professionals to analyze traffic patterns and identify malicious behaviours. Effective methodologies often incorporate a structured approach, starting with preparation and identification of relevant evidence, followed by collection, preservation, and analysis. Maintaining a clear chain of custody throughout this process is essential to ensure that the evidence remains admissible in legal proceedings and helps build a stronger case against cybercriminals.

Creating a thorough forensic analysis capability within an organization not only enhances incident response but also reinforces the overall security landscape. Regularly updating the skills of cyber security personnel in forensic techniques is vital. Continuous training in emerging tools and methodologies ensures that teams are well prepared to respond to new and evolving cyber threats. Establishing partnerships with forensic experts or external consultants can further augment internal resources, providing organizations with real-time insights and the ability to react swiftly to incidents. A proactive stance in forensic readiness can significantly mitigate the impacts of incidents, emphasizing the importance of integrating forensic principles into the broader security strategy. For organizations seeking to gain the support of executives and decision-makers, showcasing the direct link between robust forensic practices and enhanced risk management can become a powerful motivator for investment in cyber security initiatives.

8.2. Utilizing Logs for Investigation

Logs serve as the backbone of any successful cyber investigation, acting as primary sources of evidence that can unveil the timeline of events leading up to a security incident. When properly collected and maintained, logs provide invaluable insights into what occurred during a breach, who was involved, and how the attackers gained access. They encompass a wide range of data points, from system access records to application transactions, and can indicate abnormal behaviours that hint at potential security threats. Understanding the critical role logs play in investigations not only fortifies the overall security posture of an organization but also helps in upholding accountability and compliance standards. Hence, establishing a robust logging framework should be a priority for cybersecurity professionals looking to enhance their workplace security efforts.

Effective log analysis involves several techniques that can uncover hidden security incidents before they escalate into full-blown breaches. Employing methods like pattern recognition and anomaly detection enables security teams to sift through the vast volumes of log data, pinpointing unusual activity that deviates from established baselines. Utilizing tools that employ artificial intelligence or machine learning can further streamline this process, allowing for real-time monitoring and faster identification of potential threats. Correlating logs from different sources also aids in revealing more comprehensive information about a security incident. By examining logs from network devices, servers, and endpoint security solutions in tandem, professionals gain a holistic view of the attack landscape, which is essential for timely and effective response strategies. Continuous log retention and periodic reviews enhance the effectiveness of these efforts, ensuring past incidents can be revisited and learned from as your organization evolves.

Leveraging logs effectively requires more than just technology; it also involves creating a culture of security awareness within the organization. Training team members to recognize the significance of logs and how to interpret them fosters a proactive stance against potential threats. Moreover, it's crucial to ensure that logs are not only collected but also stored securely and are readily accessible for analysis when necessary. Regularly reviewing logging policies and procedures can help adapt to emerging threats, keeping your cybersecurity protocols agile. Implementing these practices not only aids in mitigating risks but also reinforces the importance of logs as critical assets in protecting your organization's digital infrastructure.

8.3. Post-Incident Review Processes

Establishing protocols for conducting post-incident reviews is crucial for improving the security posture of any organization. After an incident occurs, whether it be a data breach, malware attack, or insider threat, it is essential to have a structured approach to analyze what happened, why it happened, and how similar incidents can be avoided in the future. This process should begin immediately following the incident, where key stakeholders, including IT security professionals, management, and other relevant personnel, gather to discuss the event in detail. Documenting everything from the incident's discovery to the resolution helps create an accurate narrative that can be referred to during the review. Using established frameworks, such as the NIST Cybersecurity Framework or the SANS Incident Handler's Handbook, can provide a solid foundation for these reviews. Regularly scheduled reviews allow teams to refine their approach and adapt to evolving security challenges, ultimately fostering a culture of continuous improvement within the organization.

Lessons learned from post-incident reviews should not remain as mere documentation; they need to inform future security strategies. By analyzing the vulnerabilities exploited during an incident, organizations can implement targeted improvements and preventive measures. This analysis may reveal gaps in current security tools, inadequate training among staff, or poor communication protocols during crisis situations. For example, if a specific phishing attack led to a breach, the organization might choose to enhance user training programs to better equip employees against such tactics in the future. Furthermore, insights gathered from incident reviews can influence the development of incident response plans, ensuring they are realistic and effective in practice. This dialogue between past events and future planning can not only bolster the security posture of the organization but also gain the buy-in of executive leadership, who are often more responsive when they see clear connections between past incidents and strategic enhancements.

Ultimately, the goal of post-incident reviews is not only to scrutinize failures but to proactively cultivate a more resilient security environment. Engaging all levels of the organization in this process ensures that insights shared are diverse and comprehensive. Regularly revisiting and revising security protocols based on actual incidents empowers cybersecurity professionals to create more robust defense's while also motivating C-level executives to invest in necessary resources. One practical tip is to schedule these reviews as regular events on the calendar, rather than waiting for an incident to occur, which keeps the importance of security awareness front and center within your organization.

9. Leveraging Threat Intelligence

9.1. Integrating Threat Intelligence Feeds

Organizations have access to various types of threat intelligence feeds that play a crucial role in enhancing their security posture. These feeds can be categorized into three main types: strategic, tactical, and operational intelligence. Strategic intelligence offers high-level insights into broader trends and threat landscapes, giving executives and decision-makers the information they need to understand potential long-term threats. Tactical intelligence focuses on specific threats and vulnerabilities that may target the organization, providing actionable insights such as indicators of compromise (IOCs) and attack patterns. Operational intelligence dives deeper into real-time data, analyzing enemy activities, ongoing attacks, and methodologies used by adversaries. By integrating these various types of threat intelligence feeds, organizations can create a comprehensive picture of their threat environment, significantly raising the effectiveness of their cybersecurity efforts.

Integrating external intelligence with Security Information and Event Management (SIEM) solutions yields numerous benefits. It enhances the detection capabilities by correlating real-time events with threat data, enabling quicker identification of potential incidents. This integration leads to more efficient incident response, as security teams can prioritize alerts based on credible threats rather than relying solely on internal baselines or heuristics. Furthermore, the incorporation of rich threat data contributes to improved investigation quality, allowing analysts to focus on genuine threats with a higher degree of accuracy. The combined intelligence also helps organizations stay ahead of emerging threats and trends, reinforcing their proactive defense rather than just reactive measures. For organizational stakeholders, including CEOs, the return on investment is evident; companies can mitigate risks, safeguard critical assets, and avoid costly breaches by leveraging integrated threat intelligence.

To maximize the impact of threat intelligence integration, it is vital to establish a robust framework for regular updates and validation of the feeds being used. Organizations should prioritize feeds that offer actionable insights relevant to their specific industry and threat landscape. Setting up automated processes for incorporation into SIEM systems can ensure that security teams are always working with the latest data, which can significantly improve response times and threat mitigation strategies. Leveraging partnerships with commercial threat intelligence providers can also enhance the value of existing security investments and offer additional layers of protection against increasingly sophisticated cyber threats.

9.2. Use Cases for Threat Intelligence

Threat intelligence plays a pivotal role in Security Information and Event Management (SIEM) operations, enhancing the overall security posture of an organization. By integrating threat intelligence feeds into SIEM systems, security teams gain insights that enable them to prioritize incidents effectively. This information allows for a contextual understanding of alerts, reducing both false positives and the workload on security analysts. For example, when a SIEM tool alerts on a suspicious login attempt, threat intelligence can quickly provide data on whether the source IP address is known for malicious activity. This capability allows security teams to respond faster and more accurately, aligning their efforts with imminent threats rather than historical data alone.

Several organizations have successfully leveraged threat intelligence to mitigate real threats. In one notable incident, a financial institution was alerted to unusual traffic patterns indicative of a Distributed Denial of Service (DDoS) attack targeting their online banking services. By utilizing threat intelligence sourced from multiple feeds, they identified the attacking IP addresses and implemented countermeasures, reducing the impact of the assault. This proactive approach not only protected their services but also minimized potential financial loses and reputational damage. Such examples showcase the effectiveness of threat intelligence in real-world scenarios, underscoring its importance in contemporary cybersecurity operations.

To maximize the impact of threat intelligence within your organization, it is advisable to establish a robust framework for continuous monitoring and integration. Regularly updating threat intelligence feeds and ensuring that your teams are trained to interpret this information can create a security culture that is agile and responsive. Incorporating feedback loops where threat insights are discussed during incident reviews can also enhance learning and preparedness, further embedding threat intelligence into the operational fabric of your cybersecurity strategy.

9.3. Threat Intelligence Platforms Overview

Several key threat intelligence platforms available in the market have gained attention for their ability to provide insights that enhance cybersecurity efforts. Platforms like Recorded Future, ThreatConnect, and Anomaly have become pivotal in the world of threat intelligence. Recorded Future leverages machine learning and natural language processing to analyze vast amounts of data, delivering real-time threat information that organizations can use to stay proactive against cyber threats. ThreatConnect integrates threat data from various sources, providing a centralized platform where analysts can collaborate and automate their response to potential security incidents. Anomaly brings a different approach by focusing on driving threat intelligence into operational environments, aiding organizations in understanding the tactics, techniques, and procedures (TTPs) of adversaries. Each of these platforms is designed to help security teams better understand the landscape of threats they face and respond more effectively.

Enhancing Security Information and Event Management (SIEM) tool effectiveness is where threat intelligence platforms truly shine. By integrating threat intelligence directly into SIEM tools, organizations can significantly improve the detection and response capabilities of their security systems. For instance, threat intelligence allows SIEM platforms to prioritize alerts based on the relevance and immediacy of threats, thereby reducing the noise generated by false positives. Moreover, with enriched contextual information about threats, analysts can respond more swiftly and accurately to incidents. Automation features powered by threat intelligence can also streamline workflows, enabling security teams to focus on higher-level analysis and strategic initiatives rather than getting bogged down in less critical alerts. In this way, threat intelligence platforms transform raw data into actionable intelligence, creating a more dynamic and informed approach to cybersecurity.

For cybersecurity professionals seeking to bolster their organization's defense's, understanding and leveraging threat intelligence platforms is crucial. It is essential to not only adopt these platforms but also to ensure that they are effectively integrated with existing security tools like SIEM. By doing so, organizations equip themselves with enhanced situational awareness and can move from a reactive to a proactive posture against cyber threats. A practical tip is to evaluate how your chosen threat intelligence platform integrates with your SIEM solution and look for opportunities to automate repetitive tasks, thereby freeing up your team to focus on strategic security improvements.

10. Measuring SIEM Effectiveness

10.1. Key Performance Indicators (KPIs)

Identifying Key Performance Indicators (KPIs) is crucial for effectively measuring the success of Security Information and Event Management (SIEM) systems. KPIs serve as quantifiable metrics that can highlight how well security measures are functioning and where improvements are necessary. For instance, metrics such as the number of detected threats, the response time to incidents, and the average time for threat resolution can provide insights into the effectiveness of the SIEM implementation. Additionally, understanding the volume of false positives and the number of alerts that lead to actionable insights enables security professionals to refine their threat detection processes. It is also essential to tailor KPIs to align with the specific goals and security frameworks of the organization, ensuring that they address the unique risks and challenges faced within the network environment.

Interpreting these metrics requires a nuanced understanding of the security landscape. Data should be analyzed in context rather than in isolation; for example, a decrease in the number of alerts may seem positive but could also indicate a lack of monitoring comprehensiveness. Similarly, monitoring the trends over time provides a clearer picture of whether security readiness is improving. Engaging in comparative analysis with historical data can illuminate patterns that demand attention, while benchmarking against industry standards offers additional perspective. Presenting these insights effectively to stakeholders, especially CEOs and upper management, is vital for gaining their buy-in for future security investments or initiatives. By using data visualization tools, security professionals can communicate complex information simply and effectively, helping to portray the narrative of the organization's security posture.

Avoiding the pitfalls of relying solely on superficial metrics is essential to enhancing an organization's cybersecurity stance. It's important to focus on comprehensive KPIs that offer real-time insights into both network and individual user security. Regularly reassessing and adjusting these KPIs ensures that they remain relevant to the evolving threat landscape and organizational objectives. As a practical tip, organizations should develop a dashboard that consolidates these key metrics, allowing for a more streamlined view of security health. This not only simplifies monitoring but also facilitates timely action and informed decision-making within the cybersecurity framework.

10.2. Metrics for Security Operations

Measuring the effectiveness of security operations is vital in today's digital landscape, where threats evolve rapidly. Various metrics exist to provide a comprehensive view of security performance, enabling teams to identify strengths and weaknesses in their security posture. Common metrics include the number of incidents detected and responded to, the time taken to identify and rectify these incidents, and the volume of false positives generated by security systems. Additionally, tracking the number of successful attacks versus attempted attacks offers insights into the resilience of the security framework. Understanding user behaviour, such as the frequency of phishing attempts reported by employees, can also reveal vulnerabilities that need addressing. These metrics, when effectively collected and analyzed, empower security professionals to pinpoint areas for improvement, optimize incident response protocols, and enhance overall organizational security management.

Beyond evaluation, the impact of these metrics on strategic decision-making is profound. The insights derived from security metrics inform the allocation of resources, influence policy adjustments, and guide the implementation of new technologies. For example, if a particular metric indicates a spike in a specific type of incident, the security team can prioritize training sessions for employees or adjust their defence's against that threat vector. Furthermore, presenting these metrics effectively to executives fosters a deeper understanding of the security landscape, allowing for informed discussions about investment and support for critical initiatives. Engaging with these metrics not only helps in immediate threat mitigation but also plays a role in long-term strategic planning, ensuring that security measures remain agile amidst an ever-changing threat environment.

For cyber security professionals, understanding how to translate metrics into actionable insights is key to ensuring ongoing organizational safety and obtaining buy-in from leadership. By establishing a clear correlation between metrics and outcomes, security teams can articulate the value of their efforts, fostering a culture of security awareness that permeates the organization. Engaging regularly with stakeholders to share data-driven stories about security performance not only strengthens the relationship between security teams and upper management but also enhances the overall security posture of the organization. Positioning metrics as a means of storytelling can greatly aid in securing necessary investments for new tools and technologies that can shore up defense's against potential attacks.

10.3. Reporting to Executive Management

Developing effective reporting methods for presenting SIEM findings to executives is crucial for ensuring that security incidents are understood in the context of the organization's broader objectives. The reports should be concise yet informative, providing an overview of incidents that have occurred, the potential impacts on business operations, and the steps taken to mitigate risks. Visual aids, such as graphs and charts, can be incredibly powerful in conveying complex data quickly. Executives are often pressed for time, so reports should focus on key performance indicators (KPIs) that align with organizational goals, ensuring that the security team's priorities are clearly linked to business objectives. Using straightforward language is important; avoiding technical jargon can help facilitate understanding and enhance engagement among non-technical stakeholders.

Discussing key insights executives should derive from SIEM reports is essential for intelligent decision-making. It is important that reports highlight not only the number and types of incidents detected but also trends that indicate potential vulnerabilities within the organization. For instance, if there is a repeated pattern of phishing attempts targeting specific departments, this warrants further investigation and possibly more robust training for those teams. Executives should be made aware of areas where the organization stands strong in its security posture versus areas that may require immediate attention or resource allocation. Furthermore, framing the findings in terms of business risk rather than just technical faults can help bridge the gap between cybersecurity efforts and executive strategy. This alignment encourages buy-in from leadership, facilitating increased support for funding and resources to bolster security measures further.

By crafting reports that focus on strategic insights and actionable recommendations, cybersecurity professionals can foster an environment where security is seen as an integral component of the business rather than a mere IT concern. When presenting findings, it's also beneficial to offer a forward-looking perspective. This could involve outlining steps for improvement or predicting future security challenges based on current trends. Emphasizing proactive measures can aid in securing leadership support for ongoing cybersecurity initiatives. Engaging executives with concise, impactful reports will not only enhance their understanding but can also lead to a more robust security culture throughout the organization, ultimately creating a safer, more resilient workplace.

11. Enhancing SIEM with AI and Machine Learning

11.1. Overview of AI in Cyber Security

AI technologies play a crucial role in enhancing cyber security measures by automating detection processes, analyzing vast amounts of data, and identifying potential threats in real-time. Traditional security methods often rely on static, rule-based approaches that can quickly become outdated in the face of evolving threats. AI, with its ability to learn from data and adapt to new patterns, provides a dynamic layer of defense. Machine learning algorithms can analyze user behaviour, flagging irregularities that may indicate a breach or compromise. This proactive approach not only speeds up threat detection but also reduces the burden on security teams, allowing them to focus on strategic rather than repetitive tasks. Furthermore, AI can assist in incident response by suggesting remedial actions based on past incidents, thus improving the overall security posture of an organization.

Current applications of AI within cyber security frameworks are diverse and impactful. For instance, AI-driven security information and event management (SIEM) systems can correlate data from different sources, providing a comprehensive view of security threats across the network. Similarly, endpoint detection and response (EDR) solutions utilize AI to monitor endpoints and respond to suspicious activities. Automated threat hunting is another area where AI shines, employing algorithms to sift through and analyze logs to identify potential vulnerabilities proactively. Additionally, AI can enhance phishing detection efforts by analyzing email content and behaviours, successfully reducing the incidence of human error. As AI continues to advance, its integration into mobile security and cloud computing will redefine how organizations safeguard their digital assets, making it essential for cyber security professionals to stay informed about these developments.

For organizations looking to leverage AI in their cyber security strategies, a practical tip is to prioritize the integration of AI tools that can enhance existing measures rather than replace them entirely. This hybrid approach allows for a smoother transition and increases acceptance among staff, while still reaping the benefits of AI-powered insights and automation. Continuous evaluation of AI performance is vital, as the landscape of cyber threats is ever-changing, and organizations must ensure their defence's evolve in response.

11.2. Machine Learning Algorithms for Anomaly Detection

Machine learning algorithms significantly enhance the detection of abnormal activities by analyzing vast amounts of data with high precision and speed. These algorithms leverage historical data to learn what constitutes normal behaviour within a network, thereby allowing them to identify deviations that may indicate potential threats. Instead of relying solely on predefined rules, machine learning models adapt and evolve, improving their detection capabilities over time. This dynamism makes them particularly valuable in a landscape where cyber threats are becoming more sophisticated. For instance, supervised learning techniques can utilize labeled datasets to train models that detect specific types of anomalies, such as unauthorized access attempts or unusual data transfers. Conversely, unsupervised learning approaches can autonomously detect novel and previously unseen anomalies by analyzing patterns and clusters, which are particularly beneficial in environments where malicious activities are not immediately apparent. This adaptability empowers organizations to respond swiftly and effectively to threats, bolstering their overall security posture.

Within Security Information and Event Management (SIEM) environments, several machine learning algorithms have proven suitable for enhancing anomaly detection. Random Forest, a popular ensemble learning method, effectively distinguishes between benign and malicious activities by aggregating results from multiple decision trees. This approach helps reduce false positives, making it easier for security professionals to focus on genuinely concerning issues. Another well-suited algorithm is Support Vector Machines (SVM), which excels in high-dimensional spaces and can classify events based on a hyperplane that best separates normal from anomalous data. In the realm of deep learning, neural networks also play a crucial role, especially Recurrent Neural Networks (RNNs) and Long Short-Term Memory networks (LSTMs), which excel in sequence prediction and time-series data. These models are adept at maintaining context, allowing them to recognize patterns over time, which is essential when analyzing logs from a SIEM system. Furthermore, clustering techniques like K-Means can aid in identifying groups of similar data points, uncovering patterns that may indicate incipient attacks. The implementation of these algorithms within SIEM frameworks can enhance the detection of security incidents and streamline the response process.

Having a clear understanding of these machine learning algorithms allows cyber security professionals to tailor their approaches to best fit their organizational needs. It's vital to continuously test and refine the chosen models to adapt to the evolving threat landscape. Organizations should also consider a hybrid approach that combines multiple algorithms to improve accuracy and reduce false alarms. By investing in advanced machine learning techniques and supporting technologies, companies can gain significant insights into their security posture, thus enabling them to protect critical assets more effectively. A practical tip is to always keep your anomaly detection systems updated with the latest data and threat intelligence, as this ensures that the models are trained on the most relevant information. This proactive approach not only enhances detection capabilities but also fosters greater trust in the systems among stakeholders and executives alike.

11.3. Future Trends in AI-Powered SIEM

Predicting how AI advancements will shape the future of SIEM tools reveals a landscape rich with potential. The integration of more sophisticated AI algorithms is expected to enhance the ability of SIEM systems to process vast amounts of data in real time. As AI becomes more adept at recognizing patterns and anomalies, SIEM solutions will not only improve threat detection but also predictive capabilities. This means that future SIEM tools could anticipate attacks before they occur, allowing organizations to proactively address vulnerabilities. The development of self-learning algorithms will enable these systems to evolve continuously, refining their threat response strategies based on past incidents and emerging trends. This shift towards predictive analytics in SIEM will not only enhance security postures but also streamline operations, thereby saving valuable time and resources for cybersecurity professionals. CEOs and decision-makers must understand that adopting these advanced capabilities is not just about staying current; it's about maintaining a resilient line of defense against increasingly sophisticated threats.

Identifying areas of growth and emerging technologies within SIEM landscapes is crucial for aligning cybersecurity strategies with business objectives. As organizations migrate to cloud environments, the need for cloud-native SIEM solutions is becoming apparent. These tools will be designed to operate seamlessly across hybrid and multi-cloud architectures, providing visibility and control where traditional systems may falter. The fusion of machine learning with behavioural analytics is another exciting development, as it allows SIEM solutions to assess user behaviour and network traffic continuously, identifying deviations that could signify insider threats or compromised accounts. Furthermore, the rise of automation through orchestrated responses means that SIEM can triage alerts and initiate countermeasures without human intervention. This proactive stance not only alleviates the burden on security teams but also ensures a faster reaction time in critical situations. Cybersecurity professionals must be forward-thinking, investing in training and technologies that align with these trends to enhance overall security effectiveness.

In looking at the horizon of AI-powered SIEM, it's essential to understand that collaboration will play a pivotal role. Integrating SIEM tools with other cybersecurity infrastructure—like firewalls, intrusion detection systems, and endpoint detection solutions—will facilitate a more holistic security approach. This integration allows for a more comprehensive view of the security landscape, enabling better context surrounding incidents as they arise. Effective communication between various security technologies will ensure that organizations respond to threats with speed and precision. For cybersecurity professionals, maintaining awareness of these trends and advocating for their adoption within their organizations is critical. Investing in relevant training, fostering a culture of security awareness, and remaining adaptable to technological advancements can significantly enhance an organization's security posture going forward.

12. Challenges in SIEM Implementation

12.1. Addressing Resource Limitations

During the implementation of a Security Information and Event Management (SIEM) system, organizations frequently encounter various resource-related challenges. One of the most common issues is the lack of adequate budget resources. Many organizations underestimate the financial commitment necessary for a successful SIEM deployment, leading to insufficient funding for essential components like software licenses, hardware infrastructure, and ongoing operational costs. Additionally, businesses may struggle with a shortage of qualified personnel who possess the expertise required to configure, maintain, and optimize the SIEM solution effectively. As threats to cybersecurity become increasingly sophisticated, the need for skilled analysts who can interpret the massive amounts of data collected by SIEM systems becomes paramount. Furthermore, organizations often face technological limitations, particularly if their existing infrastructure is outdated or incompatible with new SIEM tools, which can hinder integration and data collection processes.

To overcome these limitations, organizations can adopt several effective strategies. First, outlining a clear business case for the SIEM investment can help secure necessary funding from stakeholders, especially CEOs who prioritize risk management within the organization. It is important to emphasize the potential return on investment by illustrating how a robust SIEM solution can mitigate risks and reduce the likely financial fallout from cyber incidents. Additionally, organizations can consider leveraging cloud-based SIEM solutions that typically require lower upfront costs and can scale according to organizational needs. This flexibility can help in avoiding overwhelming initial resource requirements. Furthermore, investing in training and development for existing IT staff can bridge the skills gap, allowing them to manage the SIEM tools more competently and efficiently. In many cases, partnering with managed security service providers (MSSPs) can also alleviate personnel shortages, providing access to cybersecurity expertise without the need for hiring permanent staff.

A proactive approach can greatly help in navigating these challenges. Regularly assessing resource needs and limitations as part of the SIEM implementation plan can prevent bottlenecks. Additionally, establishing a phased rollout allows organizations to allocate resources more judiciously and adjust to operational demands incrementally. A focus on aligning the SIEM system with the organization's larger security strategy ensures that it will be effectively utilized and supported, rather than becoming an underused tool in the cybersecurity arsenal.

12.2. Avoiding Common Pitfalls

Implementing Security Information and Event Management (SIEM) solutions can be a game changer for organizations seeking to bolster their cybersecurity posture. However, many organizations still stumble due to frequent mistakes made during implementation. A common error is neglecting to define clear objectives before deployment. Without specific goals, teams may struggle to discern whether their SIEM investment is delivering value. Additionally, inadequate integration with existing systems can lead to a fractured security landscape, reducing the overall utility of the SIEM tool. Overlooking the importance of user training is another critical pitfall. If staff members are uninformed about the system's capabilities or how to respond to alerts, the potential for effective threat mitigation decreases significantly. Finally, there is often a tendency to over-rely on automated processes. While automation is a powerful feature of SIEM tools, the human element remains crucial in interpreting data and making critical decisions in response to threats.

To avoid these pitfalls, organizations should take proactive measures that establish a solid foundation for their SIEM implementation. Start by creating a clear roadmap that outlines specific objectives and success metrics, which will help teams measure progress and adjust strategies as necessary. It is equally essential to ensure that the SIEM system is compatible with existing infrastructure to allow for seamless integration. This collaborative approach enhances the efficiency of detecting and responding to threats. Organizations must invest in comprehensive training programs that empower employees to fully leverage the capabilities of the SIEM solution. Regular workshops and practical simulations can build confidence and competence in responding to alerts effectively. Additionally, fostering a culture that values continuous improvement and feedback will help bridge the gap between automated threat detection and human oversight, ensuring that security teams are well-prepared to make informed decisions based on the data provided.

As a practical tip, consider conducting a post-implementation review after deploying your SIEM system. This review should analyze performance against the set objectives, gather feedback from users, and identify any ongoing challenges. Regular assessments will not only help in fine-tuning your approach but will also demonstrate a commitment to maintaining an adaptive and responsive security posture.

12.3. Managing Change Resistance Within Teams

Addressing human factors that lead to resistance against SIEM deployments requires a fundamental understanding of the psychology within teams. Resistance often originates from fear of the unknown, lack of trust in new systems, and the discomfort that comes from changing established routines. When Security Information and Event Management (SIEM) systems are introduced, team members may worry about their job security or feel inadequate in their skills to manage a new tool. It's essential to foster an environment where concerns can be openly discussed, allowing for transparency. Engaging team members early in the deployment process can help mitigate these fears, as individuals feel included and valued. By conveying the benefits of SIEM, such as enhanced security posture and improved incident response capabilities, you can align team goals with the objectives of the deployment, encouraging cooperation.

Developing communication and training strategies to facilitate acceptance is critical for successful SIEM implementation. A comprehensive communication plan should ensure that all team members are informed about the purpose of the SIEM system and how it aligns with the organization's goals. Regular updates and open channels for feedback can build trust and address misinformation. Training is equally essential, as it equips staff with the necessary skills to navigate the new system confidently. Consider creating tailored training sessions that cater to different skill levels and learning styles, which can help reinforce knowledge and reduce apprehension. Alongside formal training, providing ongoing support through mentorship or access to resources can further empower team members, fostering an atmosphere of continuous improvement and collaboration.

To effectively manage change resistance within teams, continuously emphasizing the long-term advantages of SIEM and celebrating small wins during the transition can help in embedding the new practices. By recognizing and rewarding engagement and success, you create positive reinforcement that encourages a collective shift in mindset. Engaging leadership support is also vital; having executives advocate for the change can significantly enhance buy-in across all levels. Remember, change is a process, not an event, and being patient while maintaining focus on positive outcomes can pave the way for a smoother integration of SIEM technologies into your organization's cyber security framework.

13. Building a Security Operations Center (SOC)

13.1. SOC Types and Functions

Understanding the diverse types of Security Operations Centers (SOCs) and their unique functions is crucial for any cybersecurity professional. SOCs can be categorized into several types, including internal SOCs, external SOCs, hybrid SOCs, and managed SOCs. Internal SOCs are operated by the organization itself, allowing for direct oversight and control. These SOCs are typically integrated within the organization's existing IT and security staff, providing a tailored approach to security that aligns with specific business needs. On the other hand, external SOCs are third-party services employed by organizations to handle their cybersecurity operations. This arrangement can be particularly beneficial for smaller companies that may lack the resources to maintain an internal team. Hybrid SOCs blend both internal and external talents, allowing organizations to manage critical security tasks while also outsourcing certain functions to specialists. Managed SOCs operate fully as an outsourced service, allowing organizations to focus on their core business operations while leaving security management in the hands of experts. Each SOC type serves a specific purpose, and their functions can range from threat detection and incident response to compliance monitoring and vulnerability management, fundamentally shaping how an organization defends itself against cyber threats.

Security Information and Event Management (SIEM) systems play a pivotal role within these SOC operational structures. SIEM solutions aggregate and analyze security data from various sources, providing security teams with real-time insights into potential security incidents. In an internal SOC, SIEM tools can enhance the ability to understand and respond to threats by correlating data across multiple platforms, resulting in quicker identification of anomalies. For external SOCs, SIEM functionalities allow third-party providers to deliver comprehensive visibility into the security events occurring within a client's infrastructure. Hybrid SOCs benefit from the versatility of SIEM, leveraging both internal resources and external expertise to enhance threat intelligence capabilities. In a managed SOC environment, SIEM is often one of the key technologies used, as it enables continuous monitoring and advanced analytics to detect and respond to threats proactively. By integrating SIEM into their workflows, SOCs not only improve their operational efficiency but also gain a significant advantage in strategizing their security posture.

To effectively enhance security within the workplace, cybersecurity professionals should prioritize selecting the appropriate SOC type for their needs and ensure that a robust SIEM system is in place. It is essential to align operational capabilities with organizational goals and consider factors such as available resources, expertise, and specific security requirements. Additionally, fostering collaboration between internal teams and any external partners can create a more united front against cyber threats. Ultimately, an informed choice regarding SOC structure and leveraging SIEM tools can significantly bolster an organization's defense strategies and overall security posture.

13.2. SIEM's Role in the SOC

Security Information and Event Management (SIEM) systems are pivotal in enhancing security monitoring within the Security Operations Center (SOC). They aggregate log data generated throughout the organization's technology infrastructure, from host systems and applications to network and security devices. As analysts sift through a wealth of data, SIEM platforms streamline workflows by offering real-time visibility and correlation capabilities. This integration allows SOC teams to efficiently prioritize incidents that demand their immediate attention, reducing the noise generated by false positives. By harnessing the power of advanced analytics, machine learning, and threat intelligence, SIEM tools facilitate proactive threat hunting and incident response, ultimately supporting the overall mission of safeguarding sensitive information and maintaining operational integrity.

The effectiveness of a SOC heavily relies on the robustness of its SIEM functionalities. A well-implemented SIEM solution not only enriches data but also empowers security analysts with actionable insights. Features such as automated alerting, incident response workflows, and comprehensive reporting enhance the team's ability to respond to threats in a timely manner. Moreover, having a strong SIEM reduces the amount of time analysts spend on mundane tasks, allowing them to focus on critical security challenges. When SIEM solutions are properly integrated into the SOC's operational framework, they provide a solid foundation for risk management and compliance efforts, further solidifying the organization's security posture.

Cybersecurity professionals should continuously evaluate their SIEM implementations to ensure they are exploiting the full potential of these systems. This might involve regular training for analysts on new SIEM features or seeking enhancements that enable better integration with other security tools in use. Engaging with stakeholders, including upper management, is essential for fostering a culture of security awareness and investment in advanced technologies. By ensuring that SIEM remains central to the SOC's strategies, organizations can better protect themselves against evolving cyber threats, making it a critical aspect of modern cybersecurity practices.

13.3. Best Practices for SOC Establishment

Establishing a successful Security Operations Center (SOC) from the ground up requires a well-defined strategy. Begin by assessing the organization's specific security needs and aligning them with the overall business objectives. A comprehensive risk assessment helps in identifying critical assets and potential threats, which will guide the development of your SOC's scope. Establishing clear objectives and measurable goals is essential to ensure the SOC remains focused on its mission. Deciding on the SOC's structure is equally important. Will it function as a centralized unit, a distributed operation across locations, or a hybrid model? Each option has its implications on communication, response time, and operational efficiency. You should also consider creating a phased implementation plan that allows for adjustments and improvements over time. Regularly reviewing and evolving this plan ensures the SOC adapts to changing threats and technology landscapes, thus maintaining its relevance and effectiveness.

Identifying key personnel is crucial for the SOC's success. The team should consist of individuals with a diverse set of skills, including incident response, threat intelligence, and forensic analysis. Look for personnel with experience in both security technologies and the specific industry in which your organization operates. This will enable the team to understand the unique regulatory and threat landscape. It's equally vital to invest in technology that supports the SOC's objectives. This includes Security Information and Event Management (SIEM) systems, threat detection tools, and incident response platforms. Integrating these technologies can enhance situational awareness, streamline operations, and improve response capabilities. Additionally, regular training and certification opportunities for SOC staff foster continuous learning and skill enhancement, which is critical in the rapidly evolving field of cybersecurity.

Collaboration between the SOC and other departments such as IT, risk management, and compliance is vital for a comprehensive security approach. Establishing well-defined communication channels can enhance the SOC's proactive monitoring capabilities and streamline incident management processes. For organizations looking to gain CEO buy-in, it's essential to present clear data and metrics demonstrating the value of the SOC in mitigating risks and protecting business assets. Building a strong case for investment in a SOC—highlighting its capability to prevent costly breaches and ensure compliance—can create the organizational support necessary for its establishment and success. As you work towards establishing a SOC, consider continually updating your approach based on industry best practices and innovations, ensuring you stay ahead of emerging threats and maintain an effective cybersecurity posture.

14. Future of SIEM and Cyber Security

14.1. Emerging Technologies in Cyber Security

Emerging technologies are reshaping the cyber security landscape, creating both opportunities and challenges for organizations. Artificial Intelligence (AI) and Machine Learning (ML) are at the forefront of this transformation. They enable advanced threat detection capabilities by analyzing vast amounts of data and identifying patterns indicative of potential cyber threats. AI can automate repetitive tasks, allowing cyber security professionals to focus on more complex issues. Similarly, Blockchain technology promises to enhance data integrity and security through its decentralized nature, making it difficult for malicious actors to alter information without detection. Quantum computing, although still in its infancy, poses new challenges, particularly in encryption. As quantum processors become more powerful, traditional encryption methods may become obsolete, prompting a re-evaluation of current security measures.

The implications of these technologies for Security Information and Event Management (SIEM) implementations are profound. With the integration of AI and ML, SIEM systems can evolve from reactive to proactive security solutions. These systems will be capable of learning from historical data and adapting to new threats dynamically. Additionally, the use of blockchain can enhance the integrity of the logs that SIEM systems rely on, ensuring that the data they analyze is trustworthy. Organizations must also consider the impact of quantum computing on their encryption strategies within SIEM solutions, preparing to adopt quantum-resistant algorithms to safeguard sensitive information. By embracing these emerging technologies, organizations can better defend their networks against increasingly sophisticated cyber threats and ensure a more robust security posture.

Understanding these advancements is essential for cyber security professionals aiming to enhance workplace security. Keeping abreast of these technologies not only helps in strategic planning but also in securing buy-in from stakeholders and CEOs who may be hesitant to invest in new solutions. As these technologies continue to evolve, leaning into them provides a forward-thinking approach to safeguarding the organization's assets. Professionals should prioritize continuous learning and adaptation to integrate these technologies into their cyber security frameworks effectively.

14.2. Predictions for SIEM Evolution

As cyber threats continue to grow more sophisticated, Security Information and Event Management (SIEM) tools will inevitably evolve to meet the challenges posed by these changes. The landscape of cybersecurity is shifting towards a greater focus on real-time threat detection and response capabilities, which has significant implications for SIEM technology. Emerging technologies such as machine learning and artificial intelligence are expected to play a crucial role in enhancing the analytics capabilities of SIEM systems. By leveraging these technologies, SIEM tools will not only improve their ability to detect anomalies but will also enable organizations to automate threat detection and response processes. This means that as threats become more complex, SIEM systems will increasingly need to incorporate behavioural analysis and predictive analytics to manage the vast amounts of security data generated across networks. The integration of such capabilities can help organizations stay ahead of threats, giving IT teams the intelligence needed to act swiftly and effectively.

In addition to advanced analytics, innovations in data integration and orchestration will also redefine SIEM capabilities. As the number and variety of security tools increase, the need for seamless integration becomes essential. Future SIEM solutions are expected to provide better integration with existing security applications, allowing for a centralized view of security incidents and events. This could lead to the development of advanced dashboards that provide actionable insights and visualizations, enhancing situational awareness for security professionals and enabling faster decision-making. Furthermore, the incorporation of cloud technologies into SIEM platforms will not only make it easier to manage hybrid environments but will also facilitate better data governance and compliance, ensuring that organizations can meet regulatory requirements while enhancing their security posture. The shift towards cloud-based SIEM solutions will also support improved scalability and flexibility, allowing organizations to adapt to changing workloads and threats dynamically.

Ultimately, the evolution of SIEM tools will be shaped by the ever-evolving landscape of cyber threats, necessitating continuous innovation in technologies and methodologies. Understanding these trends can provide cybersecurity professionals with the insights they need to make informed decisions about their security strategies. Investing in SIEM solutions that prioritize automation, integration, and advanced analytics will not only enhance security measures within organizations but also secure CEO buy-in by demonstrating a proactive approach to risk management. As cybersecurity threats continue to advance, being at the forefront of SIEM evolution will be critical for achieving effective and resilient security operations.

14.3. Preparing for Future Threat Landscapes

Organizations today face an increasingly complex array of threats that can emerge from both technological advancements and shifts in the geopolitical landscape. To remain resilient against these future threats, businesses must embrace adaptive strategies that not only respond to existing vulnerabilities but also anticipate potential issues before they escalate. This means leveraging data analytics to predict trends and employing a robust framework of cyber hygiene that permeates the organizational culture. Every team member, from the C-suite to entry-level employees, should be engaged in ongoing cybersecurity training to ensure they are equipped with the knowledge to identify phishing attempts, secure their devices, and uphold best practices when accessing organizational resources. By fostering a culture of resilience that adapts to change, organizations can better withstand the unforeseen challenges of tomorrow.

A proactive approach to risk management is fundamental in safeguarding the organization against the evolving threat landscape. This entails conducting regular vulnerability assessments, penetration testing, and risk analyses to identify weak points before adversaries can exploit them. Establishing a continuous feedback loop allows cybersecurity professionals to adjust their strategies based on real-time data and threat intelligence. Moreover, integrating cybersecurity into the overall business strategy not only emphasizes its importance but also secures buy-in from executive leadership. When CEOs understand that safeguarding digital assets directly impacts the bottom line, they are more likely to support investment in advanced security solutions and training programs. This proactive mindset effectively positions the organization not just as a reactive defender, but as a formidable player in the cybersecurity arena.

Ultimately, engaging in scenario planning and red teaming exercises can significantly enhance an organization's preparedness for future threats. By simulating potential attack vectors, cybersecurity teams can find and plug gaps before they become exploitable. Additionally, reviewing and updating incident response plans regularly ensures that the organization is primed to react swiftly and effectively in the event of an incident. A well-prepared organization will not only withstand attacks but also emerge stronger and more informed. Organizations should create a habit of learning from near-misses and incidents alike, allowing them to refine their approach continually. One practical tip is to consistently evaluate security measures against global threat reports and trends, ensuring that the organization is not only keeping up but also staying ahead.

15. Case Studies in Cyber Security Threat Mitigation

15.1. Analyzing Successful Implementations

Reviewing case studies of organizations that successfully implemented Security Information and Event Management (SIEM) tools reveals critical insights that can guide future initiatives. For example, a financial institution that faced persistent cyber threats turned to SIEM solutions to enhance its security posture. By leveraging real-time monitoring and advanced analytics, the organization was able to detect anomalies and respond to incidents with unprecedented speed. This case illustrates that careful selection of SIEM tools, paired with comprehensive training for the security team, is instrumental in maximizing the performance of such systems. Close collaboration between IT and security teams facilitated a seamless integration of these tools, ensuring that security protocols were adhered to across the organization.

Extracting best practices from their experiences highlights several key themes that all cybersecurity professionals should consider when planning similar implementations. First, establishing a clear set of goals and objectives before selecting a SIEM tool can drastically improve alignment with the organization's security needs. Organizations that thrived post-implementation often reported ongoing stakeholder engagement, particularly involving upper management. This buy-in from executives not only solidified funding for the implementation but also encouraged a culture of security awareness throughout the organization. Additionally, regular audits and continuous improvement practices allowed these organizations to adjust their security strategies based on emerging threats and vulnerabilities, keeping them one step ahead of adversaries.

Fostering a collaborative atmosphere between departments can significantly enhance the overall efficacy of SIEM implementations. Engaging not only the IT department but also operations, compliance, and risk management ensures that all perspectives are considered. This holistic approach can help create tailored solutions that fit the unique requirements of the enterprise. Furthermore, investing in ongoing education and training for all staff members, not just security personnel, can cultivate a vigilant workplace where everyone plays a role in organizational security. Establishing a clear communication channel for reporting security incidents fosters an environment where every employee understands the importance of their contribution to the security framework.

15.2. Lessons Learned from Breaches

Analyzing notable security breaches reveals critical shortcomings that organizations must address. Take the Equifax breach, for instance, which exposed the personal information of nearly 148 million individuals. The attackers exploited a known vulnerability in the Apache Struts framework, fundamentally highlighting the risks of outdated systems and insufficient patch management. Many organizations fail to prioritize regular updates or vulnerability assessments, leaving their systems vulnerable to exploit because they believe their environments are secure. Similarly, the Yahoo breaches, which allowed unauthorized access to over three billion accounts, illustrate a lack of coherent incident response planning. Security teams often found themselves unprepared when faced with significant incidents, leading to delayed responses and greater impacts than necessary. The lessons learned from these breaches urge organizations to adopt proactive security measures, including trained incident response teams and regular system audits.

Improvements in threat detection and response capabilities are essential for organizations aiming to fortify their defence's. Implementing advanced detection systems that utilize machine learning and behaviour analytics can significantly enhance the ability to identify anomalies and potential threats before they escalate. Organizations should focus on automating incident response protocols to reduce reaction times and minimize threat impacts. A well-crafted playbook can streamline responses to common incident types, allowing teams to act swiftly and effectively. Additionally, fostering a culture of continuous improvement and learning through post-incident reviews enables security teams to adapt their strategies based on evolving threat landscapes. Investment in employee training programs that emphasize recognizing phishing attempts and secure practices further bolsters the organization's overall security posture.

To enhance security and minimize breaches, organizations should adopt a layered security approach. This involves integrating various technologies and practices, such as multi-factor authentication, encryption, and regular employee training. By making security a priority across all levels of the organization, from executives to frontline employees, a culture of vigilance and responsibility can be cultivated. Using real-time monitoring tools and threat intelligence feeds will also facilitate a robust security architecture. It is not just about having the right technology in place but ensuring that all employees understand their role in maintaining security. Regularly scheduled security drills can reinforce this mindset and prepare staff to respond effectively to potential threats.

15.3. Key Takeaways for Professionals

Essential insights gathered from various case studies can provide invaluable guidance for cybersecurity professionals. Each case study highlights not just the vulnerabilities exploited, but also the strategic responses that led to successful outcomes. Professionals can learn the importance of maintaining an adaptive mindset regarding security protocols, recognizing that a static approach is often insufficient in the face of rapidly evolving threats. These studies emphasize the significance of threat intelligence and constant risk assessment across the network. Understanding how previous breaches occurred and the impact of different defensive measures can inspire innovative solutions tailored to specific environments. For instance, some organizations benefited from investing in endpoint detection and response tools, which helped them quickly identify and isolate compromised devices, limiting damage and data breaches.

Encouraging continuous learning and adaptation is crucial for cybersecurity professionals aiming to enhance security within the workplace. The rapid pace of technology and the corresponding shift in cyber threats necessitate that professionals remain informed about the latest trends and tactics employed by cyber adversaries. Engaging in ongoing training, attending industry conferences, and participating in workshops can provide insights that are applicable to real-world scenarios. Furthermore, embracing a culture of collaboration and information sharing within teams and across different organizations can lead to the development of more robust security strategies. This community approach not only fosters a knowledge-sharing environment but also increases collective awareness, diminishing the chances of falling victim to emerging threats.

As professionals delve into real-world outcomes, they are reminded that preparedness is a journey rather than a destination. Regularly revisiting and reevaluating security measures based on current data and trends will ensure that security practices are not only effective but also relevant to an organization's unique landscape. Staying proactive in threat monitoring, incident response planning, and employee training empowers cybersecurity teams to mitigate risks efficiently. By embracing a proactive stance and fostering an organizational culture committed to cybersecurity, professionals can significantly strengthen their defence's and gain the buy-in of CEOs who prioritize security as a vital business component.

www.ingramcontent.com/pod-product-compliance
Lightning Source LLC
Chambersburg PA
CBHW080605060326
40689CB00021B/4943